I0177958

Matt Kemp

True Blue Baseball Star

SportStars
Volume 1

SportStars
Volume 1

Matt Kemp

True Blue
Baseball Star

By
Christine Dzidrums
& Leah Rendon

Creative Media Publishing

CREATIVE MEDIA, INC.
PO Box 6270
Whittier, California 90609-6270
United States of America

If you purchased this book without a cover, you should be aware that this book is stolen property. It was reported as "unsold and destroyed" to the publisher, and neither the author nor the publisher has received any payment for this "stripped book."

The scanning, uploading, and distribution of this book via the Internet or via any other means without the permission of the publisher is illegal and punishable by law. Please purchase only authorized electronic editions and do not participate in or encourage electronic piracy of copyrighted materials. Your support of the authors' rights is appreciated.

The publisher does not have any control and does not assume any responsibility for author or third-party website or their content.

www.CreativeMedia.net

Cover and Book design by Joseph Dzidrums
Cover photo by Ed Ruvalcaba / PRK / PRPhotos.com

Copyright © 2013 by Creative Media, Inc. All rights reserved.
Printed in the United States of America.

First Edition: July 2013

Library of Congress Control Number: 2013912513

ISBN 978-1-938438-25-7   10 9 8 7 6 5 4 3 2 1

For Jared,
A Sweet Boy Who Likes To Read

Table of Contents

"Sometimes you have to listen to your parents. I did that, and I'm glad."

Pre-Game

On September 23, 1984, in Midwest City, Oklahoma, Carl Kemp and Judy Henderson became the proud parents of a handsome baby boy. They named their child Matthew Ryan Kemp, but everyone simply called him Matt.

When Matt was four years old, his father introduced him to baseball. Carl had played the sport while studying at Langston University, a small college in Oklahoma.

Whenever Matt played baseball, he imagined an announcer called his name as he walked to the batter's box while a pretend crowd cheered wildly. The youngster waved the bat impatiently while waiting for a pitch. When the baseball reached home plate, Matt swung forcefully, smiling at the cracking sound the bat produced as it made contact with the ball.

Matt liked watching the baseball sail gracefully through the air, before landing softly in a patch of grass. Then he zipped around the bases so fast that wind whizzed past his ears. The young player often pumped his fist as he rounded the infield, imagining he had smashed a home run in Game Seven of the World Series.

Matt also watched baseball on television all the time. Since Oklahoma didn't have a major league baseball organization, the youngster adopted the Atlanta Braves as his favorite team. Caps, jerseys and pennants celebrating the team from

Georgia cluttered his small bedroom. Inspirational quotes from baseball legends, like Tommy Lasorda, Jackie Robinson and Satchel Paige, also lined the youngster's bedroom wall.

Young Matt admired three baseball players in particular. He liked Gary Sheffield, a nine-time All-Star power hitter, for his aggressive offense. He also idolized center fielder Ken Griffey Jr., whom he considered the game's most compete player. The baseball icon earned seven Silver Slugger Awards for his brilliant hitting and snagged ten Gold Glove awards for near-flawless fielding efforts. Finally, he admired first baseman and designated hitter Frank Thomas, a two-time MVP with incredible home run power.

One day Judy bought Matt an Atlanta Braves warm-up suit. The youth grinned widely when he wore the outfit. Matt often wondered how it might feel to wear a real baseball uniform. He had no idea that he would find out one day!

Ken Griffey Jr.
(Roy Betancourt / PR Photos)

Mom and Matt
(David Gabber / PR Photos)

"Never give up on your dreams."

Chapter One

1st Inning

Although Matt excelled at baseball, he loved basketball, too. The NBA may now boast the Oklahoma City Thunder, but that team did not exist during the youngster's youth, so he rooted for the Los Angeles Lakers. Some afternoons the basketball enthusiast wore out his voice cheering for the dynamic duo of Shaquille O'Neal and Kobe Bryant. He dreamed of one day watching a Lakers game at Staples Center, the team's home arena.

Eventually, Carl and Judy ended their relationship. Although the two no longer lived together, they remained friends. As a result of his parents' split, Matt began living with his mother and grandmother full-time. Meanwhile, Judy worked two jobs as she began nursing school to build a better life for her family.

Matt greatly admired his mother's strong work ethic. Despite her hectic schedule, she remained active in his life. The devoted mom rarely missed her child's sporting or school events. Growing up, Matt found himself closer to his mother than his father.

"I wish (my dad) could have been there more," Matt later recalled to *Yahoo! Sports*. "It happens, but now we're closer. People change. We worked through that. My dad's there now."

When Matt was ten years old, his little brother Carlton entered the world. A few years later the younger sibling was diagnosed with autism, a brain disorder that makes it difficult for the person to communicate or deal with everyday events. Matt saw firsthand the challenges the disease presented and vowed to one day help bring attention to it.

Three years later the family suffered a devastating tragedy when Judy gave birth prematurely to a baby named Tyler. The preemie weighed only one pound, one ounce. Burdened with underdeveloped lungs, Tyler was unable to breathe on his own,

Midwest City High School
(Joseph Dzidrums)

so he remained in the hospital for many months while a ventilator provided air into his windpipe.

During this stressful time Matt became more independent, while his mom stayed at the hospital with ailing Tyler. He walked to school by himself, cooked many of his own meals and completed homework without anyone's prompting.

Although Tyler lived far longer than any doctor predicted, he could not completely overcome the immense challenges associated with his premature birth. Shortly after his first birthday, he passed away. The brave child left a strong impression on his family's heart, though. When Matt got his first tattoo several years later, he did so in his late baby brother's honor. His left arm bears a cross with Tyler's name, surrounded by a dove, roses and angels.

Midwest City High School
(Joseph Dzidrums)

"He was a strong baby," Matt recalled to *ESPN*. "That's all I remember. I swear that motivates me to be better than I am."

Some of Matt's favorite childhood memories involved his extended family, including his many cousins. The close relatives often gathered at his grandmother's house and spent the afternoon playing sports. The cherished tradition taught him the importance of family.

By the time Matt reached Midwest City High School, he played varsity baseball and basketball. In the latter sport, he had a teammate named Sheldon Williams who would one day play for the NBA. During Matt's junior year, the talented duo helped lead their basketball team to a state championship.

Midwest City High's Baseball Diamond
(Joseph Dzidrums)

As a result of his high-profile success, many college recruiters contacted Matt regarding basketball scholarship possibilities. However, the talented athlete declined several offers, including one from University of Oklahoma. He had really blossomed on the baseball diamond and opted to focus on that sport instead.

Craig Troxell, Midwest City High School's baseball coach, predicted a great future for Matt just mere seconds after meeting him. As he watched the young player take batting practice, he assessed his large frame, quick bat speed and immense power.

"He's going to play pro ball," Craig told another coach.

Despite his blazing talent, Matt often found himself defending his pursuit of baseball. His friends constantly teased him about his involvement in the sport.

"Where we come from, a lot of African-American players don't play baseball," he shrugged to *ESPN*.

When Matt was eighteen years old, baseball scouts began attending his high school practices and games. The young ball player mistakenly believed they represented local colleges hoping to offer him a scholarship. In reality, the professionals were pursuing him for a Major League Baseball contract!

"What are all these scouts doing here?" he finally asked his coach one day.

"They came to see you," Craig replied. "There's a possibility you could get drafted in baseball."

The revelation floored Matt. Sure, the high school student loved playing baseball, but he did not realize that it might one day lead to a high-profile career.

"I had no idea you could get drafted out of high school," he later laughed to *ESPN*.

During Matt's senior year, he hit .436 with 8 home runs and 52 RBIs. Even more impressively, the ball player cultivated a reputation as a five-tool player, meaning he excelled at running, hitting, power, throwing and fielding. Baseball teams crave that rare specimen - an athlete with excellent speed, big home run potential, a graceful glove and pinpoint throwing precision.

One scout in particular kept a watchful eye on the talented player. Dallas-based Mike Leuzinger, who worked for the Los Angeles Dodgers, visited Midwest, Oklahoma, in the spring of 2003. He watched several Bombers' practices and noticed something very impressive about Matt. Long after practices ended, the dedicated ball player remained alone on the field, hacking balls off a tee.

Over the next few weeks, Mike attended several Bombers' games to watch Matt. The team's standout player showed remarkable, if undeveloped, talent. Sometimes the aggressive hitter smashed several home runs in a single game, but on other occasions, he struck out in every plate appearance. Still he packed a powerful swing, possessed great speed for a power hitter and had graceful defensive skills. The kid might be a future baseball superstar, and the scout was willing to take a gamble.

On June 3, 2003, Major League Baseball held their annual amateur draft. Using a conference call system, representatives from both leagues selected the players they wanted on their team. Thanks to Mike's prompting, the Dodgers chose Matt as their 6th round pick. Other players selected that session included his future teammates: Andre Ethier (2nd round, Oakland A's), pitcher Chad Billingsley (1st round, Dodgers) and Andy LaRoche (39th round, Dodgers).

On the day after the draft, Mike visited Matt's home. The scout handed the prospect and his parents a brochure for Dodgertown, the team's spring training site in Vero Beach, Florida.

"He showed us where I'd be staying," Matt told *The New York Times.* "I had never been to the beach. I was excited about getting away from home and seeing how it was."

MIDWEST CITY HIGH SCHOOL

ALL-STATE▪

AJ HINCH	92	JASON SUDIK	97
MATT MYERS	92	RYAN BUDDE	98
BRAD JACKSON	93	TOMMY WHITEMAN	98
PAUL CRANFORD	93	KEYSTONE HUGHES	03
DALE PEARSON	95	JEREMY McBRYDE	05
GARRET BELL	95,96	RYAN KILMER	06
VERNON MAXWELL	95,96	ANDREW THIGPEN	07
GREG BRUNO	12		

PLAYER OF THE YEAR

▪JOHN VOSSEN	48	▪TED COX	73
▪BREWSTER HOBBY	56	▪RONNIE GOOCH	75
▪GARRY WEESE	68	▪JIMMY LONG	82
▪HAROLD TOMPKINS	69	▪KEVIN ATKINS	83
▪JOE SHADDIX	70	▪CURTIS WINGO	84
▪BOB SUELLENTROP	71	▪MIKE GUNDY	86
▪JIMMY BLAIN	72		

GATORADE NATIONAL PLAYER OF THE YEAR

▪MITCH SIMONS	87	▪RODNEY FOSTER	90
▪EUGENE MYERS	89	▪CALE GUNDY	90
▪BRANDY CANTRELL	89	▪JEREMY WOODS	91

ABCA ALL AMERICAN TEAM

▪DANIEL MEELEY	08
▪BRENT WEAVER	03
MATHEW KEMP	03

Midwest City High School Baseball Diamond
(Joseph Dzidrums)

On behalf of the Dodgers, Mike offered the young ball player a $100,000 dollar signing bonus. Matt rejected the first offer, though. Although it was more money.than he had ever seen, every cent mattered to his family. The astute high school senior knew he could earn a better contract.

The high-profile scout phoned his boss for permission to offer the slugger more money. In the end, Matt signed a bonus worth $130,000 dollars!

It was time to pack his bags. Matthew Ryan Kemp was now a professional baseball player.

"I want to be the best center fielder who ever played this game."

Chapter Two

MINOR LEAGUE

In late 2003, Matt began his professional athletic career in minor league baseball's rookie level. Playing for the Gulf Coast Dodgers, Matt lived in Vero Beach, Florida. He loved the picturesque coastal town with friendly inhabitants.

Former Major League player Luis Salazar managed the rookie athletes. The 2003 roster included five ball players who would eventually play in the big leagues: Tony Abreau, Lucas May, Russ Mitchell, Travis Denker and Matt Kemp. The young team played at Field One, the historic diamond where Sandy Koufax pitched his first professional game.

Matt played 42 of 60 games for the Gulf Coast Dodgers. He hit a modest .270 and collected 43 hits in 159 at-bats. The amazing phenom even helped his team finish second in the Eastern division.

The following year Matt hopped over to the neighboring state to play for the Dodgers' Class A affiliate, the Columbus Catfish in Georgia. Managed by Dann Bilardello, a former big league catcher, the Catfish's roster included future teammates Hung-Chih Kuo and Andy LaRoche. The nineteen-year-old recorded 17 home runs, 8 triples, 22 doubles and a .288 batting average.

In 2004-05 Matt nabbed a roster spot on the Vero Beach Dodgers in the Class A Advanced league. Wearing number 84, the twenty-year-old loved playing the team's home games at Holman Stadium, which also served as Los Angeles' notable

Dodgertown
(Joseph Dzidrums)

spring training facility. He even passed Adrian Beltre's franchise record for home runs (27), netted 90 RBIs, 76 Runs and 23 stolen bases. For his impressive accomplishments, he was selected to the 2004 Florida State League All-Star team.

Playing professional baseball afforded Matt the opportunity to see many parts of the United States. He traveled to tourist destinations like Charleston, North Carolina; Daytona Beach, Florida; and Savannah, Georgia. Despite the enlightening traveling, Matt still felt homesick. He had never lived away from home and missed his family greatly. The close-knit group made daily phone calls to ease the difficult transition.

In 2006 Matt graduated to Class AA ball with the Jacksonville Suns. He was now just two levels away from the major leagues. Under manager John Shoemaker, the determined outfielder carved a strong season by hitting 7 home runs and knocking in 34 RBIs in just 48 games. The club even announced that he would receive his own bobblehead doll on June 23rd. Yet when that momentous occasion arrived, the popular player was nowhere near the Florida stadium, and for good reason.

On Saturday, May 27th, Dodger personnel called Matt into their office. The eager player hoped he was being promoted to the team's Class AAA Las Vegas team. Only the surprised ball player learned that he would bypass the next level entirely. Instead he would next play for the Los Angeles Dodgers.

Matt Kemp was heading to the big leagues!

Dodgertown
(Joseph Dzidrums)

"With baseball, you have to stay humble. It's a humbling game."

Chapter Three

MAJOR LEAGUE BASEBALL

The Dodgers needed help. Veteran Kenny Lofton required rest and outfielder J.D. Drew was injured, so they turned to Matt Kemp for assistance. Not only was the twenty-one-year-old on a hot streak, he could play all three outfield positions. In less than 24 hours, the kid from Oklahoma would wear a Los Angeles Dodgers uniform.

Upon hearing news of his promotion, the excited player called his mother. Soon Matt's family members were booking plane tickets to Washington, D.C., where the Dodgers would face the Nationals. When Carl's plane landed in D.C., his ex-wife Judy was already there. The proud parents would sit side by side as their son made his big league debut.

Matt shook his head in disbelief when the Dodgers' team bus pulled up to RFK Stadium. In a few hours, he would take the field as a Major League Baseball player. His new teammates included several All-Stars, like Nomar Garciaparra, Rafael Furcal, Jeff Kent and Brad Penny.

Moments later the overwhelmed player sat in the visitor's locker room holding his uniform in his hands. He ran his index finger over his last name stitched on the back of his jersey. The rookie savored the experience of buttoning up his blue and grey uniform for the first time.

After Matt dressed in his Dodgers uniform, he looked at that day's starting roster created by manager Grady Little. He would bat sixth and play center field. The youthful lineup featured a staggering six rookies.

	Rafael Furcal SS
	Jose Cruz Jr. RF
	Nomar Garciaparra 1B
	Olmedo Saenz 3B
	Willy Aybar 2B
	Matt Kemp CF
	Andre Ethier LF
	Russell Martin C
	Jae Seo P

At 1:05 p.m. on a beautiful 85-degree day, Matt Kemp officially became a Major League Baseball player. His debut got off to a rocky start, however. During the second inning, baseball's newest rookie faced World Series champion pitcher

Ramón Ortiz. He stepped into the batter's box before a crowd of 30,348 fans and struck out swinging. The fifth inning proved even more painful when he struck out again and then committed an error in the bottom half, costing the Dodgers a run. In the top of the sixth, Matt struck out a third time.

Right before his final at-bat in the 8th, Matt gave himself an internal pep talk. He would be aggressive, like his hero Gary Sheffield, but he also needed to exercise patience, like his other idol Frank Thomas. With runners on first and second, the upstart faced towering 6'11" relief pitcher Jon Rauch, the tallest player in Major League history. When the ball sailed over home plate, Matt timed his swing perfectly and popped a single, advancing his two teammates on the base paths. When he reached first base, Dodger coaches summoned for the ball.

The newest Dodger now owned a nifty souvenir marking his first Major League hit.

Although the Dodgers eventually lost the game, it was an afternoon that Matt would always cherish. His mother and father wouldn't forget the day either. Both parents nearly wore out their vocal chords cheering for their son.

"This is awesome," Carl told *The Daily Oklahoman*. "He's a big-league player now. I have no words right now, just being here at the game watching my son on the field of dreams."

"It's unbelievable," he added. "But it's real life."

"I was pretty nervous," Matt admitted. "It was a little bit frustrating at first, but in my last at-bat I got my first hit under my belt, so I'm good."

"It was just a beautiful thing," he continued. "It was fun, something I dreamed of ever since I was a little kid."

Immediately following the game, Matt and his teammates boarded a charter flight to Georgia. The young outfielder grew up idolizing the Atlanta Braves, and now he would play in their home ballpark. Batting in the fifth position, he enjoyed a stellar Memorial Day by going two for three, collecting three RBIs and scoring three runs.

During that historic game Atlanta Braves announcer Don Sutton provided the inspiration for Matt's now famous nickname. As the 6'3" 225-pound athlete stole second base with blinding speed, the commentator remarked that he looked like a "big buffalo running around the bases." Internet users tickled by the moniker altered the description to "The Bison."

Matt continued making a strong impact with his ball club. In his first six games, the rookie hit .345 with 4 home

Matt Singles In A Run
(Ed Ruvalcaba / PRK / PR Photos)

runs and 10 RBIs. He also became the first Dodger ever to hit four homers in his first ten games.

The Los Angeles Daily News stressed in late May, "Matt Kemp, arguably the club's top offensive prospect, needs to play as regularly as possible."

After a lengthy road trip, the Dodgers returned to Los Angeles for a home stand. Matt would play his first game at legendary Dodger Stadium, one of America's oldest and most beautiful ballparks. The celebrated stadium hosted such notable baseball moments like Sandy Koufax's 1965 perfect game and Kirk Gibson's 1988 World Series home run.

"[Dodger Stadium is] without a doubt the nicest stadium I've ever played in," Matt told *The Daily News*. "And the biggest, of course."

When the young ball player arrived at the clubhouse for his Dodger Stadium debut, veteran pitcher Derek Lowe pulled him over to the batting lineup posted on a wall. Matt now hit in the number two position.

"You're moving on up in the world," Derek joked. "You're like George and Weezie from the TV show *The Jeffersons*. 'Movin' on up.'"

Matt laughed at his teammate's silly comment. Then in his second at-bat that night, the slugger smashed his first big-league home run.

"Definitely a special feeling," Matt smiled afterward.

A few days later, Matt's mother, grandmother, uncle and two aunts arrived in Los Angeles. The exhausted but excited family had piled into a van and driven nine hours straight to watch their favorite athlete play at Chavez Ravine, site of

Dodger Stadium. L.A.'s newest outfielder welcomed his relatives to the City of Angels with his own personal fireworks display, hitting two monster home runs in the same game.

"I'm still on cloud nine right now," the red-hot player told *The Associated Press*. "I'm feeling good, I'm seeing the ball well, getting good pitches to hit, and they're going out of the ballpark. I'm glad I'm helping my team win. I'm surprised I'm up here, but I'm glad."

"He is still behind the bigger names on the Dodgers, yet he is producing with more consistency," raved the *Los Angeles Sentinel*. "Kemp has been the head of the Dodgers recent scoring boon reaching base in every game he has started."

Dodger manager Grady Little raved about Matt's playing ability. On one occasion he compared the rookie's potential to superstars Chipper Jones and Joe DiMaggio. Such grand praise might inflate a ball player's ego, but the Oklahoman remained grounded.

"I just want to make a name for myself," he told *The Daily News*. "It's nice to be compared to players like that, but I haven't done anything compared to them."

Once the scorching summer days of July arrived, though, Matt's bat cooled off. He struggled mightily, managing only 4 RBIs, striking out 41 times and posting a meek .216 batting average.

On July 14th, the Dodgers optioned Matt to their Class AAA team, the 51s. The organization believed the talented youngster, might regain his swing while playing in Las Vegas. Instead of whining or complaining, Matt expressed gratitude for the opportunity to play in the majors.

Million-Dollar Smile
(David Gabber / PR Photos)

"It was a great feeling," he told *The Oklahoman*. "Being in the big leagues was something I dreamed about since I was a little kid. I got a chance to play and help the team win."

"It hurts to be sent down," he added. "You don't want to be in the minor leagues, but that's life. I've just got to work on some things for the long run."

Although Matt felt disappointed to return to the minors, he quickly transformed his frustration into a positive experience. The determined athlete went on a hitting spree in Nevada after he focused on hitting the ball to the opposite field.

As the playoffs neared, top Major League Baseball teams scrambled to strengthen their roster. Several teams, including the Boston Red Sox, approached the Dodgers with offers to purchase Matt's contract. Los Angeles personnel balked at any deals, though. They carried big expectations for their top prospect. The Oklahoma native wasn't going anywhere.

On September 1st, when Major League active rosters expanded from 25 players to 40, Matt received the long-awaited phone call. He and his 51s' teammates James Loney and catcher Einar Diaz were going to Los Angeles.

"I'm ready to do whatever they need," Matt announced.

The focused slugger scored a run in his first game back in the majors. Matt flashed a huge grin nearly all night. It felt terrific being back in the big leagues. Specifically, he was thrilled to be wearing a Los Angeles uniform.

"This is where I want to be," Matt told *The Daily News*. "I want to be a Dodger."

"I want to stay here. This is home. I can't see myself playing for anybody else. I only know blue."

Chapter Four

STARTING LINEUP

Determined to prove he belonged in the major leagues, Matt arrived at 2007 spring training a week earlier than most position players, The focused athlete spent the extra seven days working on his defensive skills by striving to catch balls faster and throwing with greater accuracy. He hoped his efforts would land him a spot on the Dodgers' opening day roster - and it did.

On the Dodgers' home opener, though, Matt suffered an unfortunate injury. In the fourth inning as he ran to catch Jeff Baker's eventual triple, he rammed straight into the auxiliary scoreboard. The frustrated player left the game with a sore right shoulder. The injury landed him on the 15-day disabled list.

"I don't want to aggravate it," Matt told *The Daily News*. "When you're (playing) hurt, you can (get into) bad habits with your swing and with throwing, and I don't want that."

"I play hard, and I guess that's what I get for playing hard," he added. "But that's just my game, and I'm not going to change."

Matt began a rehabbing assignment with the Dodgers' Class AAA team. When the organization activated him from the disabled list, they kept him in Las Vegas so he would get as much playing time as possible. The disappointed player moved into an apartment with his good friend Delwyn Young and set his sights on returning to Los Angeles.

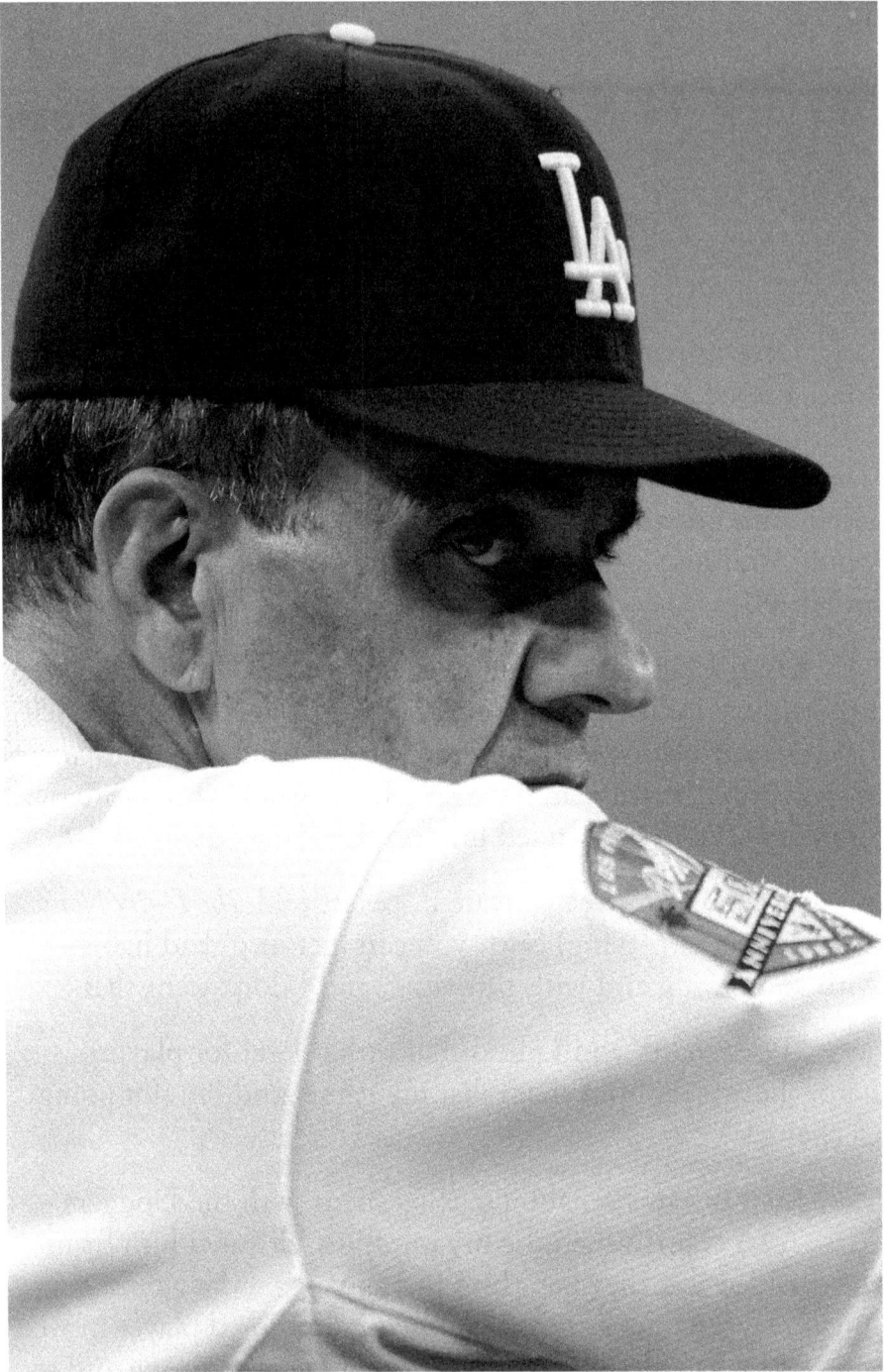

Manager Joe Torre
(Ed Ruvalcaba / PRK / PR Photos)

Not surprisingly, Matt's bat went ablaze in the minor leagues. He hit .329 with a 14-game hitting streak. When the Dodgers recalled the player, he vowed to remain in the major leagues for good.

On June 8, 2007, Matt returned to Dodger Stadium as a pinch runner. In late August, he recorded his first four-hit game. In the end, the focused player finished the season with a .342 batting average, 10 home runs and 42 RBIs.

Despite a strong, gifted team, the Dodgers missed making the playoffs. Many baseball experts, along with General Manager Ned Colletti, expressed concern with Grady Little's management decisions. On October 30, 2007, the beleaguered skipper announced his resignation. The organization needed a strong presence that would guide the team back into the playoffs and help young players, like Matt, fully realize their potential. They found the answer in a baseball legend named Joe Torre.

When the Yankees' former manager arrived in Los Angeles, he inherited an embarrassment of riches. In fact, Joe's overabundance of strong players provided an enviable problem. The Dodgers had four outstanding outfielders but only three regular positions: five-time All-Star Andruw Jones, speedy leadoff hitter Juan Pierre and two hot prospects, Andre Ethier and Matt. The Oklahoman refused to let the fierce competition weigh him down.

"I can only control what I do," he told *The Daily News*. "If I take care of business, everything else will take care of itself."

In March of 2008, Matt, several teammates and his new manager flew to Beijing on an 18-hour flight to play the San Diego Padres in Major League Baseball's first ever game in China. The trip was designed to introduce the country, who would host the summer Olympics in less than five months, to America's pastime.

A crowd of 12,224 fans filled the seats at Wukesong Stadium to watch game one. The historic event got off to an awkward start when Chinese spectators struggled to understand the sport. Thousands cheered for foul balls, while most sat silently during the usually rousing "Take Me Out to the Ballgame."

Matt used the rare opportunity to take in the country's many breathtaking sights. His favorite outing centered on visiting the Great Wall of China. Matt also promoted the sport to Chinese citizens by embarking on a media tour.

"Anytime you can stimulate interest in the game, that's a good thing," Joe Torre remarked.

When the Dodgers left Brooklyn, New York, and arrived in Southern California in 1958, the team played their home games in the historic Los Angeles Coliseum while awaiting Dodger Stadium's completion. On March 29, 2008, in honor of the team's 50th anniversary, workers transformed the monstrous venue back into a baseball stadium for a Dodgers' exhibition game against the Boston Red Sox. The sell-out game drew the largest baseball crowd in U.S. history. Sports enthusiasts snatched up 90,505 general admission seats and 25,000 standing-room-only tickets.

Manny Ramirez and Matt Share a Laugh
(Ed Ruvalcaba / PRK / PR Photos)

When the regular season began, upstarts Matt and Andre produced steady numbers to become regular fixtures in the starting lineup. Andruw Jones struggled, though, leading the Dodgers to acquire superstar Manny Ramirez for his mighty bat. The new Dodger's carefree demeanor and monster home runs rejuvenated Los Angeles. The regular outfield rotation became Manny as the left fielder, Andre managing right field and Matt in center field, his favorite position.

"It's cool out there," he told *The Daily News*. "I can play all three (outfield positions). I guess I'm more comfortable in center field."

When a reporter asked Matt if Manny had breathed life into a once quiet clubhouse, the outfielder's trademark smile lit up his face, as he shook his head incredulously.

"Where have you been, man?" he laughed.

The Dodgers ended up winning their division title, sending them into the postseason. In their first playoff round, the team defeated the Chicago Cubs to advance to the National League Championship Series. Yet in the end, they narrowly missed making the World Series, losing to the Philadelphia Phillies in five games.

Regardless of the outcome, when Matt reflected on his first full season in the big leagues, he had to be happy. The twenty-four-year-old was now a starting player on the Los Angeles Dodgers. He ended the season with solid stats: 93 runs, 176 hits, 35 stolen bases and a .290 average.

And his best years were still to come!

Carlton and Matt
(Ed Ruvalcaba / PRK / PR Photos)

"It's a joy to be known as a Dodger."

Chapter Five

BASEBALL STAR

Matt's second full year in the majors eclipsed his first. His .297 batting average, 26 home runs, 101 RBIs, and 34 steals helped lead the Dodgers to a Western division title. In the playoffs, though, they lost in the second round to the Philadelphia Phillies.

Once the season officially ended, Matt won a pair of prestigious awards. He nabbed the Gold Glove award for his stellar defense in the outfield and the Silver Slugger for being the best offensive player in the league at his position.

When 2010 rolled around, Matt was a legitimate baseball star, and the Dodgers' most productive hitter. For his tremendous accomplishments, the slugger received a substantial salary raise. The added financial security meant the world to him.

"I've been working hard since I was a little kid to get to this point," he proclaimed. "I'm happy. It's big for me and my family. I get to do some great things for them now."

If Matt had become a big star on the baseball diamond, he also began making waves off the field, too. The center fielder began dating popular recording artist Rihanna. Everywhere the photogenic duo went, media followed. After about a year of dating, though, they ended their relationship but remained friends. They even met for dinner on a few occasions to catch up with one another's lives.

Matt also worked with various charity organizations. His top priority involved bringing more attention to autism. He partnered with TACA (Talk About Curing Autism), an organization dedicated to educating, empowering and supporting families affected by autism. The ball player worked tirelessly to educate others on the disease that affected his brother Carlton.

The L.A. Dodger also kept his deceased brother Tyler in his heart, too. After every home run he hit, when his foot touched home plate, Matt pointed to the sky in acknowledgement of his beloved sibling.

"That's a tribute to him and what he means to me," the outfielder remarked.

Matt and His Teammates Jump for Joy
(Ed Ruvalcaba / PRK / PR Photos)

"I wish he were still here," he continued. "He'd be 14 right now. He'd be a big kid. He'd be coming out to baseball games and in the locker room with me, hanging out. He's with me on that baseball field when I go out there and play every day. I'm always talking to him out there in the outfield. We have long conversations."

In his free time, Matt enjoyed the laid-back Southern California lifestyle. At first the enormity of Los Angeles overwhelmed him, but once he became more acquainted with the city, he loved it. The ball player's new surroundings even helped broaden his culinary tastes. For years he refused to try sushi, but because the dish is omnipresent in the City of Angels, the reluctant eater finally tried it and quickly became a big fan!

On most mornings, Matt started his day with a bowl of cereal while watching television. On days he felt like getting fresh air, he headed to his favorite restaurant, Vivian's Café in Studio City, for scrambled eggs and pancakes. On days off he donned purple clothing, drove to Staples Center, grabbed his favorite dish from California Pizza Kitchen and cheered on the Lakers.

When Matt preferred quiet time, he relaxed in front of his big screen television. He felt especially inspired after watching the popular miniseries *The Bible*. Each week he also looked forward to enjoying his favorite weekly show *Suits*, a USA Network drama about a fictional New York City law firm.

The music lover even began guitar lessons. Matt liked many different musical genres, but he particularly adored R&B, old school or new school. However, his diverse CD collection included a large sampling of styles, like Young Jeezy, Rick Ross, Jay-Z and Gucci Mane.

"Music can make you happy, it can make you mad," he told *LA Weekly*. "It makes me happy. It calms me before a game."

Naturally people felt curious about Matt's love life. As one of sport's most eligible bachelors, people often asked him what he looked for in a woman.

"I like confident people. I like positive people," he revealed to *Flaunt Magazine*. "Somebody that makes me want to be a better person. Smart. Pretty, of course. Somebody that is close with their family and loves their family just as much as I love my family. Somebody that knows how to dress. It just boils down to being confident and being comfortable in your own skin and the person that you are."

Matt's favorite lady would always be his mother, though. Upon finding big-league success, he moved his mom to Los Angeles so she could attend every Dodgers home game. The doting son also pampered his mom with manicure appointments and trendy hair salon visits.

"I moved her out here to LA to keep an eye on me, to keep me out of trouble," he smiled. "I take care of my mom."

Of course, Matt spoiled himself, too. The fashion-conscious ball player always wore stylish clothing. At one point, he owned over 400 pairs of shoes! Yet if the Dodgers were on a winning streak, the superstitious star refused to change his socks for fear of jinxing his team. Sometimes he wore the same pair for nearly two weeks!

And if Dodger fans had their way, the only color socks that Matt would ever wear would be Dodger blue socks. They adored their star center fielder, and soon the world would fall in love with him, too.

Matt and Kelly Johnson Play Ball
(Ed Ruvalcaba / PRK / PR Photos)

"When I'm in center field and I see 56,000 people screaming and hollering and cheering... that probably is one of the best feelings in the world."

Chapter Six

SUPERSTAR

The 2010 season was difficult for Matt. Although he started off the year red-hot, including seven home runs in the month of April, he faltered in the second-half of the season and finished the year with just a .249 average.

Dissatisfied with his production the previous season, Matt was determined to turn things around in 2011. The center fielder faced a lot of changes going into the season. For starters, first-time manager Don Mattingly took over as skipper for the Blue Crew after Joe Torre retired in 2010.

The Dodgers also acquired a new first base coach, former Dodger Davey Lopes. Although Matt was blessed with natural speed, the 2010 season had been disappointing on the base paths. He was caught stealing bases 15 times. It was time to sharpen his base-running skills. With more than 550 career stolen bases to his name, Lopes was the ideal teacher.

The two worked closely during spring training, with Lopes helping Matt perfect his timing. After just a few weeks of helpful tips and lessons, Matt fully believed he could steal 40 bases during the upcoming season.

"Out of 40, I don't want to ever get thrown out," he declared to the *Los Angeles Times*.

After completing spring training in Glendale, Arizona, the Dodgers started a new season on March 31, 2011, at Dodger Stadium under the bright blue Southern California skies. Los Angeles faced their heated rivals that day, defending World Series champions, the San Francisco Giants.

Matt exhibited a lot of patience at the plate on Opening Day, garnering three walks and a hit during his four at-bats. He also had a stolen base! The Dodgers won 2-1 behind the strong pitching effort of ace Clayton Kershaw.

Success continued for Matt throughout the season's first full month. In April, the big masher hit two game-winning home runs, one in the 9th inning off the St. Louis Cardinals and another in the 12th inning against the Atlanta Braves.

Matt was proud of his strong start to the season.

"Last year is behind me now," he relayed to *ESPN*. "I'm mentally tougher now. I hope I can stay consistent and get better and better every year."

Unfortunately, there was turmoil for the Dodgers off the field. Owner Frank McCourt fought to maintain control of the team despite personal and financial problems. The media bombarded players with questions about the ownership's woes.

Matt didn't let the distractions get to him, however. Instead he stayed focused on his role as the starting center fielder. While some in the media thought the tumultuous off-field activities would cause some players to question their commitment to the Dodgers, Matt remained loyal. He made it clear that he had no interest in being traded or signing with another team during the off-season.

"This is where I want to be. I was drafted by the L.A. Dodgers. I can't see myself playing for anybody else," Matt declared on the TV sports talk show *Jim Rome Is Burning*.

In spite of the off-field commotion, Matt's bat continued to heat up. By mid-July he was hitting .313 with 22 homers and 67 RBIs. Many players dream of impressive stats like that at the end of the year. Matt racked up those huge numbers at just the halfway mark of the season!

Baseball experts began speculating that Matt might get to play in his first All-Star Game, a prestigious annual event that pits the best players in the American League against the top players in the National League. The starting lineup for both teams is picked by fans who cast millions of ballots, ultimately voting for the players they deem most worthy of the honor.

On July 3rd, while Matt anxiously awaited the results of the All-Star balloting, he logged on to his *Twitter* account to kill time. Oddly enough, one of his thousands of followers broke the good news – the fans selected him as a starting outfielder for the All-Star Team! Dodgers starting pitcher Clayton Kershaw and outfielder Andre Ethier also made the squad.

One week later, Matt arrived in Phoenix at Chase Field, home stadium to the Arizona Diamondbacks and site of the 2011 All-Star Game. Matt was still brimming with excitement when he received a precious memento from his father. It was a photograph of the first ballpark Matt ever played in – a Little League diamond in Midwest City.

"It just hit me," a pensive Matt told the *Los Angeles Times*. "It reflected where I was and how far I've come."

An enthusiastic Matt couldn't believe he was at the All-Star Game, rubbing elbows with such great players as Derek Jeter, David Ortiz and Chipper Jones.

Matt Walks The Red Carpet At The ESPYs
(Allen Berezovsky / PR Photos)

"This is all happening so fast," he exclaimed. "I'm really excited. It didn't hit me until this morning, when I was having breakfast with all the guys."

"I'm just in awe right now."

If being selected for the team wasn't enough of an honor, Matt would also participate in the Home Run Derby. The good-natured competition takes place the day before the All-Star Game and is reserved for baseball's top power hitters. Whichever player hits the most home runs that evening is deemed the champion. Matt was thrilled to be invited.

"I've been watching it since I was a kid and I've always dreamed of being in one," Matt explained to *MLB.com*.

"I remember watching Frank Thomas, Ken Griffey Jr., all the big hitters on TV. Every kid likes the Home Run Derby."

Although Matt only hit two home runs in the derby and finished in last place, he still had fun. He also received some great news that day. Bruce Bochy, manager of the Giants and the National League All-Star Team, announced that Matt would bat third in the lineup the following day. He was stunned. On a team full of exceptional athletes, the Dodger center fielder was picked to hit in the spot typically reserved for the squad's best player.

"Unfortunately I see too much of him, being in our division," Bochy explained to the *Los Angeles Times*. "He's a guy with speed and power; a guy that can beat you with a base hit or the long ball. He's what you call a complete player."

The night of the All-Star Game, Matt excitedly took to the field in Phoenix. In his two at-bats, he had a single and a walk. The magical experience was topped off by the fact that the National League won 5-1!

With the All-Star break over, Matt continued his torrid hitting pace throughout the second half of the season. On August 26th, he hit his 30th home run of the season, becoming only the second Dodger player to hit at least 30 homers and steal at least 30 bases in one season.

Matt reflected on his spectacular season on *The Jim Rome Show*.

"I'm just having fun, concentrating and not trying so hard. When I try to do too much, the results don't end up the way I want. I just have to trust in my ability."

"I'm trying to have more consistent at-bats," he continued. "I'm going up there with a plan and sticking with that plan. I'm studying the game more and seeing what pitchers are doing to me."

Matt realized that being selective at the plate was crucial for a successful season – a fact he struggled with in the past.

"Sometimes I get impatient at the plate and I end up swinging at bad pitches. Now I wait for good pitches to hit and when you get good pitches to hit, you usually get pretty good results," he laughed.

In spite of these major adjustments, Matt also realized that it was important to maintain his upbeat personality.

"I'm still the same old guy. I'm just having a lot more fun," he told *Mighty 1090*. "I'm just trying to make everyone loose around here and make them smile. I just want to go out and win some baseball games!"

As the season progressed, Matt's hard work continued to pay off, including all those one-on-one sessions he spent with Davey Lopes during spring training. In mid-September, Matt's early season prediction came true when he got his 40th stolen base!

Although the Dodgers fell short of making the playoffs, finishing in third place in their division, Matt ended the season with 39 home runs and 126 RBIs. In fact, he led the National League in both categories!

Running the Bases
(Ed Ruvalcaba / PRK / PR Photos)

Superstar
(Koi Sojer / PR Photos)

In the post-season accolades, Matt won the Hank Aaron Award, given to the best hitter in the National League. He then narrowly missed winning baseball's most coveted honor, the National League Most Valuable Player Award, when he finished second to fellow outfielder Ryan Braun of the Milwaukee Brewers. Some baseball critics felt that Braun won the MVP Award because his team advanced to the playoffs that year, while the Dodgers did not. Whatever the reason, Matt was happy for Braun and his accomplishments.

"Ryan's a special player," proclaimed Matt on *The Jim Rome Show*. "He's had a heck of a season, too. He's one of my favorite players. I enjoy watching him."

The Dodgers wanted to reward Matt for his spectacular season and make certain that he remained in Los Angeles for as long as possible. In November, the two sides agreed to an 8-year, $160 million contract extension. It was the largest contract the Dodgers had ever given a player!

Dressed in a snazzy suit and bow tie, Matt beamed with pride as he and the Dodgers announced the new contract.

"I love this city, the fans and just to be a part of this as a Dodgers player. I definitely want to spend the rest of my career here," Matt told *MLB.com*.

"Like Derek Jeter with the Yankees, I would like to spend the rest of my career here and be part of a dynasty. We have the opportunity to have something special here."

"I want to win as many games as we can and get to the World Series. It is a great city and a great organization to be a part of."

"I'm just living a dream."

Chapter Seven

VETERAN

Following Matt's dream season, he became the unofficial face of the Los Angeles Dodgers. The popular player traveled everywhere making promotional appearances on behalf of his beloved team. His popularity continued to soar with his official *Twitter* account reaching 315,000 followers!

Fittingly enough, the two loves of Matt's life merged on March 28, 2012, when a group that included former Lakers great Magic Johnson purchased the Los Angeles Dodgers. The NBA legend was an icon in the sports world, and particularly in Los Angeles. The Dodgers center fielder couldn't have been happier about the purchase.

"Good day 4 the @dodgers," he tweeted. "The great @ magicjohnson is the new owner!! Let's start a dynasty baby!!"

Shortly after the new ownership went into effect, Matt chatted with the Laker great. He left the conversation feeling invigorated and inspired.

His excitement showed on the field, too. The undisputed Dodger leader was consistently the hero of well-fought games. In 2012 he became the only player in Major League Baseball history to win National Player of the Week three straight times. Fittingly enough, in that same season, he broke hero Gary Sheffield's Dodger record for most home runs hit in April. He accomplished the impressive feat with a dramatic walk-off smash at Dodger Stadium. Upon shattering the record, he embraced his teammates. Afterward the loving son jogged over to the stands to embrace his proud mother.

"It's definitely emotional, and it makes me play better," Matt told *MLB.com*.

"I've played with a lot of great players, but this guy is as good as it gets," raved veteran teammate Jerry Hairston Jr.

Prior to the start of the 2013 season, Matt underwent shoulder surgery. Despite his physical obstacles, the resolute athlete notched his 1,000th career hit that year. Fittingly enough, he reached the major milestone on Mother's Day.

"She's my hero, and I look up to her," Matt remarked.

If Matt built a reputation for his stellar baseball playing ability, he also garnered attention for his renowned generous spirit. In early May, he and his team arrived at AT&T Park to play their arch rivals, the San Francisco Giants. Mere minutes after the Dodgers were swept in three games, third-base coach Tim Wallach approached Matt with sad news. A big Dodger fan named Joshua Jones sat by the third-base line. The teenager's father had informed him that his son was battling cancer and only had weeks to live. His favorite player? Matt Kemp.

Touched by the story, the Dodger superstar sprinted over to meet his ailing fan. He shook the young man's hand, autographed a baseball for him and gifted him several souvenirs:

his Dodger cap, game jersey and cleats. Unbeknownst to Matt, Joshua's friend Tommy videotaped the kind act and later uploaded it to the Internet video-sharing web site *YouTube*. The clip went viral overnight, touching those who watched it. News stations and sports networks even ran the clip several times. When Matt awoke the next morning, dozens of voice messages cluttered his cell phone.

"What did I do now?" he wondered.

After listening to his first message, Matt realized that the private moment had gone public. Suddenly everyone wanted to speak to him about his touching gesture. By the time he arrived at Dodger Stadium for a night game, the team had arranged an impromptu press conference just to accommodate all the media requests.

"I didn't plan on taking my jersey off. It was just something I felt that probably would have cheered him up a little bit and helped his situation," Matt told *The Associated Press*. "It was the first time I ever took my shoes off on a field. That was the first time that Giants fans were ever nice to me."

The Dodgers also hoped that his generous act would inspire his peers to also treat their fans with the utmost respect. As a twelve-year-old, Matt was snubbed by his favorite basketball player, and he never forgot how much it stung. When the Oklahoma native became a famous athlete himself, he promised to always treat fans kindly.

"I don't think some athletes understand what they can do with a simple gesture and how big it is, just shaking a kid's hand or saying "Hi" to him," he stressed. "It can make a fan's day - or a fan's life."

"Life is so much bigger than baseball," the All-Star continued. "You think about going 0 for 4 with 4 Ks and you get mad, and you can complain about the stupidest things some-times. Things like this humble you and keep you grounded and let you know that somebody's life is way worse than whatever it is you've got going on."

Every time Matt took the field, he always counted his many blessings. He felt grateful for a wonderful family, an enormous talent, good health and loyal fans. The All-Star still felt like a child when he played baseball. Whenever the umpire signaled the start of a game, excitement and enthusiasm soared through his body.

"We have a lot of fun out there," the much-loved player grinned. "It's a kid's game. I've been playing since I was four years old. I'm going to keep having fun and laughing."

And with those words, the baseball veteran raced eagerly on to the field to play ball.

An LA Presence
(Joseph Dzidrums)

Essential Links

Matt's Official Twitter Account
https://twitter.com/therealmattkemp

Matt's Official Facebook Account
https://facebook.com/pages/
The-Real-Matt-Kemp/425129550842068

Matt's Official Instagram
http://instagram.com/bmdc27/#

Matt's Official Web Site
http://www.therealmattkemp.com/

Dodgers Official Web Site
http://www.dodgers.com

Official Major League Baseball Web Site
http://www.mlb.com

Kemp's Kids
http://therealmattkemp.com/kids/

Talk About Curing Autism Web Site
http://www.tacanow.org/

About the Authors

Christine Dzidrums has written biographies on many inspiring people: Yasiel Puig, Mike Trout, Matt Kemp, Clayton Kershaw, Joannie Rochette, Yuna Kim, Shawn Johnson, Nastia Liukin, The Fierce Five, Gabby Douglas, Sutton Foster, Kelly Clarkson, Idina Menzel and Missy Franklin.

Christine's fictional works include: *Cutters Don't Cry*, (Moonbeam Children's Book Award), *Fair Youth*, *Timmy and the Baseball Birthday Party*, *Timmy Adopts a Girl Dog*, *Future Presidents Club* and *Princess Dessabelle Makes a Friend*.

Leah Rendon graduated with a Bachelor of Arts degree from the University of California, Los Angeles. She coauthored the children's biographies *Joannie Rochette: Canadian Ice Princess*, *Shawn Johnson: Gymnastics' Golden Girl* and *Jennie Finch: Softball Superstar*. The Southern California native also contributed to the tween book *Fair Youth*.

Build Your SkateStars™
Collection Today!

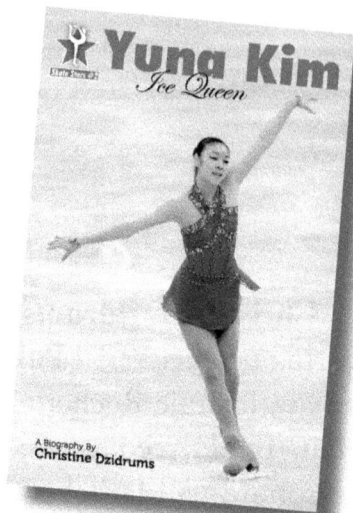

At the 2010 Vancouver Olympics, tragic circumstances thrust **Joannie Rochette** into the spotlight when her mother died two days before the ladies short program. Joannie then captured hearts everywhere by courageously skating two moving programs to win the Olympic bronze medal.

Joannie Rochette: Canadian Ice Princess profiles the popular figure skater's moving journey.

Meet figure skating's biggest star: **Yuna Kim**. The Korean trailblazer produced two legendary performances at the 2010 Vancouver Olympic Games to win the gold medal. *Yuna Kim: Ice Queen* uncovers the compelling story of how the beloved figure skater overcame poor training conditions, various injuries and numerous other obstacles to become world and Olympic champion.

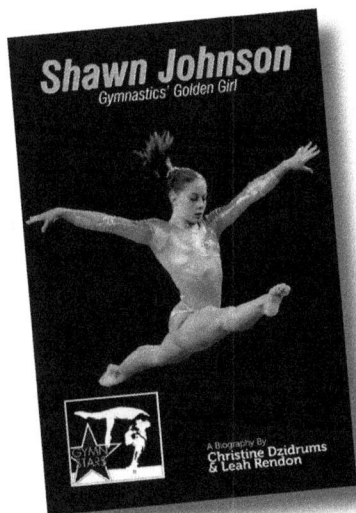

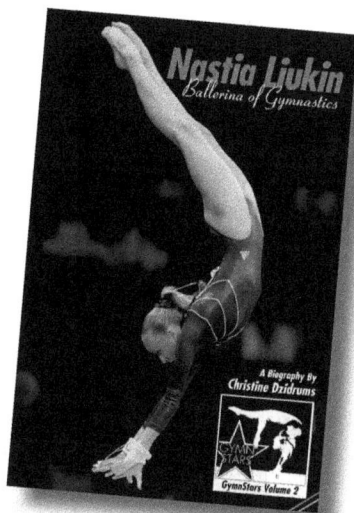

Shawn Johnson, the young woman from Des Moines, Iowa, captivated the world at the 2008 Beijing Olympics when she snagged a gold medal on the balance beam.

Shawn Johnson: Gymnastics' Golden Girl, the first volume in the **GymnStars** series, chronicles the life and career of one of sports' most beloved athletes.

Widely considered America's greatest gymnast ever, **Nastia Liukin** has inspired an entire generation with her brilliant technique, remarkable sportsmanship and unparalleled artistry.

A children's biography, *Nastia Liukin: Ballerina of Gymnastics* traces the Olympic all-around champion's ascent from gifted child prodigy to queen of her sport.

Also From

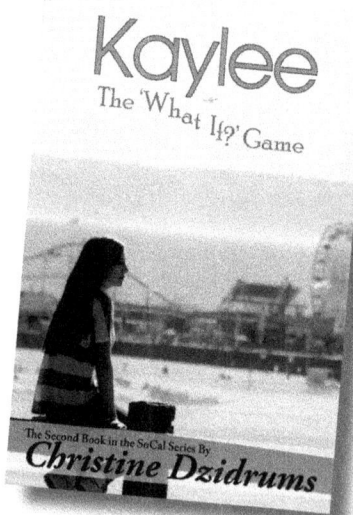

2010 Moonbeam Children's Book Award Winner! In a series of raw journal entries written to her absentee father, a teenager chronicles her penchant for self-harm, a serious struggle with depression and an inability to vocally express her feelings.

"I play the 'What If?'" game all the time. It's a cruel, wicked game."

When free spirit Kaylee suffers a devastating loss, her personality turns dark as she struggles with depression and unresolved anger. Can Kaylee repair her broken spirit, or will she remain a changed person?

Creative Media Publishing

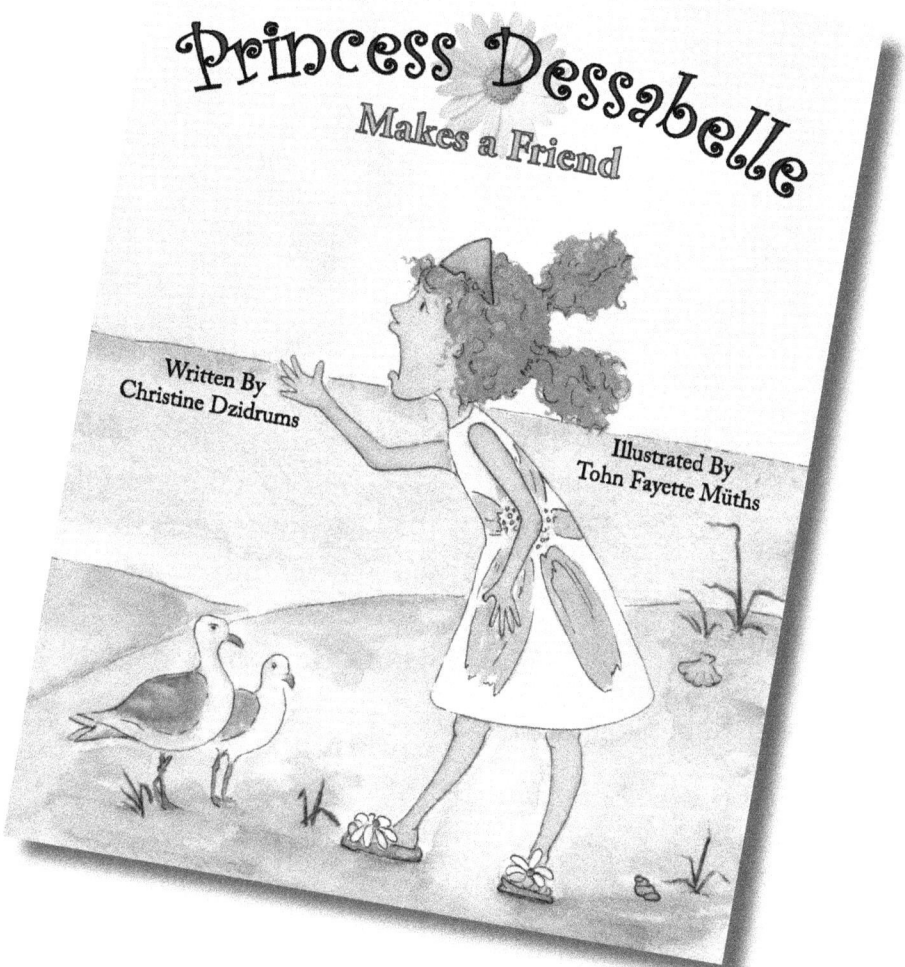

Meet **Princess Dessabelle**, a spoiled, lonely princess with a quick temper. When she orders a kind classmate to be her friend, she learns the true meaning of friendship.

Build Your Timmy™
Collection Today!

Meet Timmy Martin, the world's biggest baseball fan.

One day the young boy gets invited to his cousin's birthday party. Only it's not just any old birthday party... It's a baseball birthday party!

Timmy and the Baseball Birthday Party is the first book in a series of stories featuring the world's most curious little boy!

Timmy Martin has always wanted a dog. Imagine his excitement when his mom and dad let him adopt a pet from the animal shelter. Will Timmy find the perfect dog? And will his new pet know how to play baseball?

Timmy Adopts A Girl Dog is the second story in the series about the world's most curious 4½ year old.

Twelve-year-old Emylee Markette feels invisible. Then one fateful afternoon, three beautiful sisters arrive in her sleepy New England town and instantly become the most popular girls at Forest Springs Middle School. To everyone's surprise, the Fay sisters befriend Emylee and welcome her into their close-knit circle.

Through it all, though, Emylee's weighed down by nagging suspicions. Why were the Fay sisters so anxious to befriend her? How do they know some of her inner thoughts? What do they truly want from her?

When Emylee eventually discovers that her new friends are secretly fairies, she finds her life turned upside down yet again and must make some life-changing decisions.

Fair Youth: Emylee of Forest Springs is the first book in an exciting new series for tweens!

www.ingramcontent.com/pod-product-compliance
Lightning Source LLC
Chambersburg PA
CBHW071635040426
42452CB00009B/1636

* 9 7 8 1 9 3 8 4 3 8 2 5 7 *